Taming the Butterfly

Taming the Butterfly

Elizabethe Kelley

Cawing Crow Press

© 2015 by Elizabethe Kelley

All rights reserved. No part of this publication may be reproduced, stored in a retrieval system, distributed, or transmitted in any form, or by any means, including photocopying, recording, or other electronic or mechanical methods now available or that may become available in the future without the prior written permission of the publisher.

For permission requests, email the publisher at:
inquiry@cawingcrowpress.com

Published by:

Cawing Crow Press LLC

Dunlo, PA

ISBN: 978-1-68264-004-3

Library of Congress Control Number: 2015955454

Visit us on the web at: www.cawingcrowpress.com

Variations of some poems in this collection found their first home in the publications listed in the Acknowledgments section provided in the final pages of this book.

Some butterfly species begin their journey far south early each spring, only reaching the Appalachian region as a second generation of a very long migration completed upon their arrival in late summer. These poems recall a similar story of generations past and present. I am grateful to all who supported my journey, including my son, to whom I attribute the title of this book; my daughter, who has taught me the real meaning of love since the moment her eyes first fluttered open; and my sister, who always helped me regain my footing when I was lost, until finally, I could see our old mountains again.

For my children, and all who have known hunger.

Contents

FIRST FORM *1*

Painted Lady 3
Remembering Aeschylus 4
Forbidden 6
No Name 8
(No one speaks of the stone building) 10
Mother Poem 12
Baraboo Circus Museum 14
Cure ~ for Adrienne Rich 16
Migrant Door 17
Chimere, Hiding His Hands 19
Last of the Lake Pearls 21
What Lies Here 23
Silence Means 25
The Nature of Light 27
Anna, did you write? 30
Our Mothers' Cookbook 32
Pantheon 33
She is Asking 35

Letter 37

Aces, Eights and Hearts 38

Lilly Lake 42

Life—Like Violence 44

SEASON *49*

Variola Fever 51

Grandmother's Road 52

Near Marble Sculptures 54

Waiting for The Antelope House Runner 56

My Way Here 58

Claw, Wing 60

Broome County Courthouse, Irelu's Song for Ilargia 61

Ithaca Commons 63

White Cross Doors 64

THE EXCITEMENT *67*

Mere Bridge 69

At Thirteen 70

Jamie, Rain Season 71

Seven Sermons of the Rappahannock 73

Breast Cancer Pleroma 75

Vigil 77

Next Door 79

After the train whistle, 2:45 a.m. 81

SEVEN POWERS *83*

Sacramento 85

Return 87

Reading 89

Time 91

Jesse 93

Carrion 94

Hierophant 96

WRATH *97*

Nymphalis Antiopa 99

Wet Cement 101

Ivan's Wake 103

Crystal Aspersoria 105

She Must Have a Name 107

Salvaged Limbs, Atlas Skeleton ~ for Ruth Stone 109

Indelible Guardian 111

Daughter, Mother, Hospital Woman, Who Wraps Our Bodies? ~ for S. ... 113

Near Munich, I was born 115

Shariah Court, Honor Killing 117

Dark Energy, Dark Matter 119

Six Finger Lakes 121

V. Priceana, The Violet Age 123

Unpacking the Bread Knife 125

On a rain drop, Morning 129

Blood Mountain 131

About the Author 135

Acknowledgments 137

I was bound, though I have not bound. I was released from a world and from the fetter of oblivion, which is transient... ~ Mary Magdalene

FIRST FORM

... Matter gave birth to a passion that has no equal, which proceeded from something contrary to nature, and there arises a disturbance in its whole body...

Painted Lady

Watercolor green, medicine glass drowning
acrylic burnt sienna eyes you will understand

if you pry up pinned corners, release
willow charcoal, secret faces, cold-pressed

cotton pentimento wings, falling carefully
to the yellow tongue and groove pine. You alone

find her veiled portrait, the church window virgin
she heard speak, the girl who listened,

the woman you now hold like sunlit cut glass
chimes on the fine, dry dust school shoes make

of the earth underneath a play yard swing, light
shadows given to the page, in gratitude,

you think, for the gesture of comfort she holds out
only for you, a soft, linen shawl.

Remembering Aeschylus

The flame rises, kindling cherry logs, dry ice
fog over the rim of the watcher's copper kettle, melting
snow to a rolling boil
even in sleep, when the unforgotten falls, drip
by drip from our heart, until
out of despair, and against our will, we look

away from the signal fire to the drift
shoulder high on either side of a walkway cleared
nearly to the street, only a stone's throw
from the bay window seat sheers
lifted to see icicled ash blonde hair battering her face
on the other side of dark roots
the color of dyed leather my hands slip through, into
new gloves my mother won't wear, warm inside
unlike her frozen bend and lift, her checkered jacket
sodden with snow, Virginia-cotton against Lake Michigan
wind and freezing rain, coating aluminum
gutters and panes, sleeting closer to that moment when

the drift will collapse, and she will turn back
to measure that thump of snow, the corridor
fallen on slate, her bare wind-bitten hands

perched on the shovel's wood handle, lidless eyes
tracing stalactite ice eaves, cold hunger
glittering link to link ice teeth above the bay window
to the chain of my own arms around my waist,

hiding the wound she devours by day, always
regenerated by night

Forbidden

It is the crack of river ice, a clothesline cut down,
one end tied around a rock tossed into the center
of a fissured web where the child and now

the rope, are swept away. It is granite ice, block
after block wedged in Virginia clay, almighty
surge, the riverbed scourge thundering mussels,

silica shale glass leaflets, pearl fragment flecks,
and a small body too heavy, submerged by wicked
arms, a current too strong, tearing apart the grip

of two small hands trying to hold on, but gone. She is
gone. It is shoes unlaced, askew in sediment, clothes
frayed, mud between toes, the terrible numb ache,

strands of hair now icicle wind chimes that lacerate
frozen cheeks and forehead until blood blurs
that question in the eyes of the red spot spider

in a wood pile, who watches and waits until only one
child climbs over swelling silt to walk home alone. It is wet

leaves under a shadow hung from the young oak branch

splintered from the dark that struggles against its own weight, kicks at nothing in a death reflex. It is the jolt of nerves severed, spine exposed, holy wind tightening

the knot until the bough breaks. That daily snap, sleet-coated limbs, split sapling twigs, the burst branches bereft, fallen behind and waiting just ahead.

No Name

The worst thing that can happen to you
is to be the one
who will not eat spaghetti with mushrooms,
the one sitting alone at the table
two hours after dark, sweating
inside a witch costume, staring down
at noxious black scabs in red sauce, looking
over to the doorbell, ghost flashlights
floating down the sidewalk, flitting
off and on that living room wall, lights
crossing sheers washed, ironed and hung
on the bay window

before he comes home,
who doesn't like mushrooms either
and throws his plate at the wall, the pasta platter
across the dinner table at your mother, while
brothers finish their plates in silence
and sneak out the kitchen door

on their way to toilet-paper the split-level house
next door, where that old bitch lives

who never gives out candy corn or fifth avenue
chocolate bars, only apples you think must be sweet
and pure, their flesh soft, before all naming
before red peel cuts the core, before
red drips down the wall, drips from the cut above
her brow and into her eyes, when

your mother crawls, wiping up the floor.

(No one speaks of the stone building)

basket weave brick
fills windows and doors
light rods and voices once opened

there is no entrance
to the clay mound now, no exit
found in the outline of the old round house

built of stone and brick
white and red walls charred black
not from the kiln but from within hearth sparks

to a rag rug burning
post and beam rough sawn pine stairs
to a cradle on the attic floor, rising among

roof trusses under a fieldstone
cupola protected by an iron trap door
fretwork long since cooled

for the sparrow
arrived from a thicket below, perched

near one low slat missing in the green shutters

hook in eye locked by the mother
who waits and watches the changing road, seasons
come and go, sparrows fly and fall.

Mother Poem

if only you could know me
just once more, long enough to listen, free
of the dark nothing, the nameless
ring at the bottom of an empty glass, bile evaporated
through pores, eye blinks
counting down
to an equal chance of lids locked shut
or a wide waterless stare.   if blood seeping
could wait under final skin, one moment, osmotic
suspension, cells rested, liquid
on liquid, lungs climbing ribs, clawing their own invisible
steel beams overcome beneath salt waters
leavening the dark belly of panic
in a capsized hull, failure, unwritten and unuttered,
one more drowning
encrypted, one more
epitaph carved on a stone coffin chiseled at birth
amid alcoves, atrophy, echoes, this writhing
that moves your skull socket eyes side
to side, the death moan, now draining
cobalt irises, now dilating
the shadow of an absence

risen again, searching beyond its pillow indentation
for an offprint
the wide empty will fill, while I stand too close, waiting
for the impossible air pocket
I'll say was hope, that is hemorrhage   is spillage   is ink.

Baraboo Circus Museum

I have no dime, so I search
sawdust on the ground
around the base of her glass booth
happy to find a singular silver glint, the perfect coin
I brush off, then I stretch tall to reach the slot
and step back to where I can see
her eyelids snap
open, looking into the crystal globe.
How am I to know
she will give me no fortune card?

She is everything I will call beautiful, silver inlaid
garnet, onyx and jasper pebble rings, heavy
sterling chain and star-wheel pendant, starling hair
and eyelashes, red silk veil, black satin
opaque décolleté and hands, painted
flesh perfect except for the jagged
painted violet porcelain cup
tea leaf stain cracked throat
I see when the gypsy looks up
dark-eyeing the circus tent turning post
where I stand watching her

mechanical ruby lips opening, until
something catches
freezes the entrance to and from
the Chahta word for wound, unwritten
inside this gypsy crypt, cardless,
caught by the lit booth, stuck
between her broken lips, suspended
in sparkling dust
where every word I will ever write
rises.

Cure ~ for Adrienne Rich

She told me
I heard one word
when I first breathed in, and this is my sentence:
to remember how the word looks
before reading and writing it over and over, until

I learn there is no translation
no sound sharp enough to barb catfish
dusted in a flour sack, pan-fried yellow in hog fat
cast-iron spit at the white kitchen wall
backsplash, sizzling skinned and gutted
but hiding

bones that hurt
without bread. I remember
the way her hand gnarled around a pencil
and the power
she said
gives as it takes from us,
but not everyone listens, and no one
who hears
can ever let go.

Migrant Door

The key to your first house
of broken teeth hides
under the bed, inside a book
your father catches you reading
after school, the shotgun
Malcolm called
language, forbidden
hardcover binding
the half-red child
in a handheld mirror, you,
who do not yet know
the history of your blood,
having learned unholy white
without words to the drum
heartbeat song
to dance away the shape changer
father, stalker, husband, blank page
offprint letters, ink
stitches on the railroad
map, double steel, welded
hinges opening cinderblock cellar door
syntax, pathetic dawn stars
falling broken

on the last step, a tree with every limb
cut off, staring
down at the body
you become
just in time to forgive.

Chimere, Hiding His Hands

Old glass teaches memory
rigid flow, almost unnoticeable
when the river you are forbidden to play near
slows, genuflects, wavering ever so slightly
before the priest takes your hand, locks

the door to the room of sunlit
cabochons, immediate prism incense, black
cassock menagerie breath, rectory curio
shelves, pressed Canary flint plantation
aperitifs, fragile Victorian ruby

slippers, depression amethyst
cranberry baskets, porcelain orchids
for the altar of an old church transient wrens
and thrushes must inhabit by now, entering
vacant transom diamond portals

to and from the wound that is God,
your father's broken house of blood and grass
blots running across schoolyard pavement
cracks, crowding around St. Bernadette's

path to the edge of Accotink Creek, where

you fall to your knees, promise
return to the child you left behind,
who becomes instead a sacred stone, washed
oblique, chosen and carried inside the walled city
skin you condemn to fire, utter destruction.

Last of the Lake Pearls

Slender yellow ripples cartwheel
across my sandals, shed
from the black walnut, last to leaf
and first to fall on this path

from shoreline to shallows
lucid to refractory depth, liquid
algae into august water

I walk across clustered shells
cutting soles, invisible
incisions, these bleeding strands

of windless ink, the city streets
in your hair, threaded words
on buoyant paper; scraps folded

leap forward then back in time
until heat and light bend auburn
to a sunlit arc, near sighted

is far, saturated eyes float

then fall to the split spectrum arch

skipping stones on the lakebed

an entire rainbow, you said,

sounds like two people

standing in a front yard, looking up.

What Lies Here

These are your mother's
dishes, soaking in soapy water, her arms
full of darned socks, her needle
up through white peter pan collar buttons
and stitching the plaid uniform skirt hem, her hands
pulling hair too tight, tying the pony tail
with a rubber band snapped and repaired in a knot.

And here are her breasts, fallen, stretch marked, lonely
terry cloth robe pockets, that key
to the liquor cabinet always in the back of her mind, his urn
on a buffet shelf, the old family name
proof labels faced out from the shelves, bottleneck dust.

Now step into the mint she planted, spreading shade
bordering moss patio walkway
helicopter seeds to sweep, uprooted
dandelions and crabgrass clumps, leaf piles, laundry
baskets carried in from the clothesline, angry man
boots and belt to retrieve from the floor, the endless
picking up of shoes, dry mud

cluttering forgotten colors

and forms, of her own standing up, slowly, climbing

the back of a chair or the stair handrail, humming

that vodka lullaby whose words she can't remember, eyes

etched into frown lines you finally understand.

Things gone all wrong can't always be made right.

Even a strong woman grows tired, sometimes broken.

Silence Means

Thunder yellow rik-rack trim, the apron
hung on a kitchen peg, flour sack
heart watermark emblem dishtowels dripping
rain down screen door patches
wired into place, each tiny frame
another hour walking away
into a night bereft
of darkness, the history of ink, dough
prints on white dust, butcher block fist
after fist kneading what must rise
only to be pushed down again. She is still
here, sitting on her grandmother's pine floor
looking through the screen
one square at a time, the way
flies search the same aluminum optic grid
for a tear large enough
to crawl through
leaving behind desperate legs, bits
of wing, forsaken ommatidia, folded
facets, compound eyes, ultra-violet
life-long bruises on a vitreous body, already
numb at five years old, watching

black lawn spiders crawl across the inevitable
ivory brocade wedding dress
hem roses just out of focus, torn
fishnet stockings, perforated lens
cloth, polishing the infinite
etymology of the word
father.

The Nature of Light

When it is too late to sleep, you give in,
get out of bed, go downstairs to begin the wait
for morning. Some nights, especially in summer,
you might as well go ahead and make coffee
without cream and sugar, Iron Kettle Farm,
Prospect Valley Lane, Broken Stone Cottage,
Homestar Inn, Kline Chevrolet, retracing the way
to the cobblestone street in Ithaca,
and the low relief bronze sculpture
of lovers embedded into a brick wall.

Look into his eyes, their carved poem says, but you
flinch when the bronze man reaches up
to touch her face. Too late for him
not to discover ribs healed awkward, vertebrae
fused, law school and wedding ring-cut
lip scars. It is the fault
of a fundamental property of light, particle
and wave colors beyond deep red and dark
violet, pain-cured skin that remembers
if you try to touch and to be touched.

There is nothing beyond those Conesus thorns
in a hedgerow, grape and poison ivy vines choking
the word at the tip of
your fingers running through his hair,
no word in the language of regret
for lavender talcum steam-ironed lace gloves
holding your own small hands on the way into
a church from years ago, where everything talks at once—
patent leather heals clicking marble, censor lid
snap, half dead lily-suffocated sweet carnation,
hymn book mold, crying infant echoes, cancerous cough—

interrupting the story of your life
he writes before you are born,

when you can almost taste the soft new gray
flannel of his embrace until the choir begins
twisting the story ending into nonsense gospel, garbled
bass, endless baskets
of cloisterless fish hauled up
from below the clay landing in his heart
dumped and stranded

on the dock where you wait, leaning over the river, lit
by an abandoned camp, fire sparks
rising up through sun streams breaking water surface
into handfuls, lifting cool comfort to swelling sunset
cheek curve mountain bruises who crawl over each other,
rising into horizon, the river running past the end
of a Frazer-lined path, where you finally understand
there is nothing left to do
but turn around and look back
at the ugly witch hazel pods, magnolia petals
on dirt, unfound bread crumbs.

Anna, did you write?

I lost my place, slipped
backward into Tidewater
mornings before rain. Your bird-veined hands
light, sift flour, knead form, rising, sing
quiet warmth to bread

valley shadow to mist
above the cold river running breathless
all the way from childhood to this pooling bend,
where I cool my bare feet, unfold the map

tucked underneath one arm, trace
red Rappahannock clay to dark Susquehanna silt.
Anna, you drew the current
to this place, where even without rain, leaves drink

heart-breakingly beautiful death
and I catch the leaves in my hand
like words on paper in an attic room,
from the voice who first whispered run away. Anna,
it was you
just near dawn, standing on the staircase landing

your long silver braids hanging
to slender waist pleats, your filigree keepsake eyes
careful as cotton gown stitches
lace-hemmed above pale-footed worry.
Forgive me, Anna, I waited too long.

Who will I become now
in this world of the lost, in the eyes of my children, where
mother means God, and we are all fallen?

Our Mothers' Cookbook

You will find instructions here, quiet
underlines and careful script, handwritten
from mother to daughter, sister
to sister, aunt, niece, grandchildren
yet to be born, smudges

of yolk, double boiler
melted chocolate, Tollhouse
cookie dough, vanilla birthday frosting, toffee
pralines, egg white-sugared fresh violets
to decorate a three-tiered wedding

cake, beautiful evidence
of kitchen table talk
around living and dead, pages
torn and taped, yellow binding stitches, red
and white check Joy of Cooking book cover

wiped clean of morning bacon grease, blue
food coloring, paring knife
slips, guarding
recipes in a language
of blade and hand, oven and apron.

Pantheon

Her father says
Be quiet.
Stop that. Finish your milk. Hurry up.
I don't have all day. Eat those eggs.
For Christ sake, sit still.

His neck is shaved. A white line
bulges below the black gloss of his barbered hair.
There is a terrible weight
to his shoulders and hands. I can't see his face

but hers is too pale, suffering
unbrushed brown curls, eyes
down as she perches on her knees
across from him in the Pantheon Diner
on Main Street, trying so hard not to look
into that picture window, where sparrows
nested in brick above
Cheevers, Hand & Angeline Attorneys

feed bread to the chipped mortar hollows, growing
delicate wings with slight offerings
of crust and crumb.

On their way out, the door rings the silver bell

hung above the hinge, and the little girl

bends down to touch

one unfeathered hatchling

fallen to the sidewalk, looks up at me once

before he drags her away.

She is Asking

Was my name called? I need
to find air; I breathe but no one looks
at invisible women, hungry
carriages. We hold back our uncut hair,
winter tangled into unsayable knots. I hear
the bald caseworker say
I hope you have some reason for quitting.
She unfolds a court order; he reads
vanishing ink. I read bruises on her forearm
and cut lips. We all close our eyes, no

one tries to listen. Even I turn
away, knowing the blank stare
of shades left open, the unbearable
fullness of light, the moon pull
of night sweat, alone
in my room where I bleed these women
through my skin, and their unbathed vodka

speaks through my clothes,
begs me to lift and carry them all
in my arms, to carry them

here to you. Just look

at our hands, empty of food, look
at our heart, empty

of who will hear, who will stand in his way.

Letter

We don burqa and beg, stitch
yellow stars before lining children up

at the train, cut her braids
before she boards the school bus,

pack the overnight bag
for visitation because New York State

Supreme Court orders it so.
It is all the same Law.

Dear God, show us
one pathway out of this narrative,

one light our eyes want not just to behold
but to follow, somewhere we might

find ourselves out of reach from
shadow fabric, skin color and stars,

holocaust and hatred, cut and sewn,
mother and daughter, scarred labia.

Aces, Eights and Hearts

Cold rain. Evidence
on a sidewalk. Yellow chalk
sunflower, name, hopscotch
body circle. Where people walk, nervous
finches take cover underneath
leafless bushes or shopping carts
pushed together in a long metal line.
Crabapple leaves shiver, some huddled
safely beneath others, who bear
the incessant drops.

What a terrible force
they know, who cannot change place
and must remain stemmed
targets of unstoppable velocity.
I remember a girl left alone for hours, building
houses with playing cards, adding on
quiet porches and side rooms, careful
stories, solitary apocrypha
stacked up to what she could not know
would be called an attic, the very small
airless place

that sometimes has no entry

no exit, no staircase, just

a fitted trap door no one likes to look at,

afraid something might be hiding up there

planning the ending that begins

as every first and last

breath must, holding up a structure

forever fragile, unable to suffer

the slightest touch, not even one

meant in kindness.

We Live Now

We live in an old Endicott-Johnson factory-worker house. I love the plaster walls, 1940 Gas Stove, heirloom backyard climbing roses. And I love my neighbor, Helen, who makes butter cookies for me whenever I carry her garbage cans down and up the driveway or take her water bill payments to the post office. When Helen leans against me, and I help her from the garden to her porch chair, Helen's translucent hands are warm, the way my mother's might be now if she were still alive.

We live on Roosevelt Avenue, where people clip summer grass straight across the edge of foundations, sweep red fall leaves from the curb, sprinkle ice-melter salt on each other's sidewalks in winter so no one falls on their way to church. Sunflower whirligigs, American flags and yellow ribbons decorate every yard, porch and telephone pole. I buy Price Chopper two-for-one egg dozens, toilet paper, bread and coffee to share. I never take Helen's two dollars and 78 cents.

I drink the coffee when I cook exactly two hamburgers, one for each child, counting two pickles left in the jar and four slices of white bread for tomorrow's Friday school lunches. Sometimes we all sit together outside in strap-repaired folding chairs, and I listen to

neighborhood stories about World War II rations and how Helen's mother bartered dairy coupons for her 24 pound wedding turkey. Lester was still alive when my children and I moved here after their father went to live on Gold Street
in Manhattan. Helen says Lester liked reading his newspaper every morning, while he waited for his children to wake up.

When he died, I baked zucchini bread, covered it carefully with foil, and quietly left it on the little wood table inside Helen's front porch.

Lilly Lake

A woman sleeps on a blanket
arranged over soft grass. Light wades
through nearby shallows, dives deep, swims
to the surface her son breaks through, climbing
the rock ledge, tugging
the waist of his suit, looking over to where
his mother does not watch him
when he dives again without knowing

that even in her sleep, breathing in this day
too clear to exhale, she sees
this exact future: his red arc leap, this perfect
pointed toe splash, all of it in that instant
he toddled close to the edge, tossed a single pebble
into the lake behind the house
where they once lived.

He is almost a man now.
But in the shade of a cottonwood
he will not remember, he crawls alongside
gentle shore waves
that pull and return her wonder

at what color and shape of wisdom
the son might choose from among those

pebbles and shells, and she lifts up
her sunglasses to the leaf shadow
wildflower black shine of his baby hair and below
her eyes, the quiet bruise turning words into water
she writes on her heart: Escape
happens exactly this way; someday
we sparkle, darken, disappear.

Life—Like Violence

First, you check to see
if your hands
can move, then your arms, then your legs.
If something catches, you
cradle the broken rib or wrist
but only for a moment, just
long enough to think: maybe
wrought iron grows
wounded marrow
into railings that lead down
stairs, to asphalt
road signs, miles and miles, into
some horizon that lies beyond
swelling gold ring
cigar brand moons orbiting
thin skin on the back of one hand, circling

like dead ashes around a bonfire
at the base of your spine
translating morning urgency

into bright black blood
spots in the toilet
you didn't scrub just right, midnight
cracked lips in the filigree framed mirror.
Yes. You have to think of iron, wrought,
and hammered fire opal red
bones and skin, hematomas
glowing until finally, you stand up, because
you can, because you must cut back
the only way you know how. So you breathe
—and breathe again, over and over
and step by step, inhale to exhale until
you can walk away.

Thimbleweed Aphasia

Nightshade. Belladonna. Amanita.
Destroying angel. Slyph. Elemental soul-less
Air-being. Syllepsis: He lost his sunglasses
and his temper. Water witch. White Admiral. Limentis

arthemis, wide-banded blue and black wings.
Whiskey John, another name for the scrabbled gray jay
hiding behind harsh vegetation and a false door
to the tomb Gauntlet, that is glove armor, attack

from all sides, running between two lines
of fool's cap paper hat men who wield wooden bats,
cast premature birth, astrological miscalculation,
intentional coyote miscarriage, circling the lost scent,

injury immobilized inside plaster wrist
falcon pair actors, splinted advance, the judge
and Godfather who estimate imprecise manuscript
margin space. I say *She will not die.*

We once lived near a manmade lake in a house
built on land the Seneca called Berry Hill. I remember

how to honor a dry riverbed. Today, I will begin.
Everyone will know what you have done.

SEASON

...out of the height and the depth of the chaos,
out of the aeons of the rulers of the sphere...

Variola Fever

There are ghosts
in this book. Catachretic tumbleweeds. Itazipcho
asking for just one more blanket
we cannot know carries invisible armies
traveling the great muddy river.

Incandescent moths linger
above the place where a woman hides one shivering
child, whose vision might save ancestors
yet to be born. Christ dancer. Sclerotic

clay paint, skin covered in white
chalk, standing alone on the long black road. No
food house for the dead, only gray Sumac
thorns, Shasta daisies, Magnolia petals

underfoot, trace Aconite, Belemnite
knife-maker ribbons flapping desperate prayers
to holy wind: Ptesanwi names the dead child
light-in-the-eyes, where-the-whole-universe-dwells.

Grandmother's Road

We near awakening
when we dream
that we dream, running with abandon,
numb to thicket thorns, stumbling
here at the edge, unable
to reach gray woman
just ahead

whose long skirts
sweep leaves
aside, and whose red shawl bead fringes
fade as she turns around and you see
her eyes rain
ten thousand lakes, bramble
blood droplets slip
down her face and arms, the slate

rock waterfall rinsed cloth
and selfless kiss she gave, portent
to a fever that is
song, death, story, memory,

word into word:

I clear the way for you
daughter, she might say.

Near Marble Sculptures

Here is the season of scarcity, the pine needle
bedding and burial place, underneath
cold evergreens, where the acorns gather and hide
after hollow ripeness breaks the hold
on each tiny stem, sending the acorns clamoring
to frozen grasses in fistfuls, the way some words fall

and scatter, leaving only one behind, whose descent
remains unnoticed, a silent letting go
with the grief, the wonder
of a final snowflake through sunlight, given
a singular embrace of its own small weight
before the shell finally falls and breaks, its gaze
landing upward, a tiny dome
unblinking like the indelible oblivion or rapture

marble eyes behold, the ancient armless perception
of facing eternity alone, the ancient knowledge
that the perfect and the last
always melt or suffer underfoot, consumed
seed cup, empty but intact, clinging to
the hunger that was its hope, having hidden nothing

for itself but a small curve of light, only to sink slowly
into thaw with the same weariness
worn by the murder of sleeping crows,
gathered by night, blanketed
by their own black wings, guarding
aged winter oak limbs, skeleton key
branches along the river

where they rest, full moon enshrouded,
blessed by nothing except brown leaves.

Waiting for The Antelope House Runner

I fail with old eagle expertise, dilute
perception, muttering sleepless
heart hunger, the ache turning its head
to spy one scuttling creature
stream-edge-mirage, meatless brown, landed
here on chipped talon watermarks, my rockwork,
the end place where a human footbridge
once crossed these falls. Now

stem and leaf crumbles
next to shed copperhead skin
I thought a living snake,
and I feel little flight left
in these wings, rain that is always only rain,
nothing and no one who aims to be in a book
that will change this world into the earth again,
unacquainted with grief, sun shining on the daughter
I turn to and say

When I am gone, look for me
here, where
Taughannock wind and water spray,

carves slippery yellow rock steps
down into this deep pool,
into the time
we took turns
holding each other up.

My Way Here

Log cabin chimney smoke.

Close your eyes
to the countless great oaks
winter uprooted, begging quietly on the mountain belly,
no more important now than pine needle limbs

unfit for burning, left behind
but listening to more trees fallen
on snow, choosing to die huddled together, one
continuous blanket, arrows in their old age, pointing
down to the roadside frozen slate and up again

to hands painted on a rock above
the river that runs beneath
all memory, where I fell to my knees before I was born,
somewhere between water and woods, understanding
too late the warning signs, reading silence in wind

only after the silence breaks.
We are what we take into our heart:
mother claws, clay skin word-prints, petroglyphs who beget
escape from falling unheard, unless we forget to die

upright, bare teeth, tear apart and eat

skinwalkers who stalk our young, offering trinkets
in return for flesh.

Claw, Wing

Tin dragonfly
pressed into the side
of a galvanized bucket, black wick
citronella, effortless nigella needle leaves
in a vase, love in a mist, almost at peace, when

Before Woman
who lives underneath
your front porch knocks hard at the boards
coming loose again. *Heya*, she says, *You there
—stop rocking and go pick them apples, yonder*

*else they all gonna
just fall to the ground.* Hear her
shuffle about, sit back down with a thump,
wonder how many years white needlepoint roses
bloom and fray, held in the very same hands

that covered the lost
daughter, slender body,
large eyes, imprinted reticular wings, delicate
tracery. She was almost a miracle,
Before Woman remembers, quietly.

Broome County Courthouse, Irelu's Song for Ilargia

I could have watched more carefully, but didn't
want to dream his face ever after.
I should have known from the scent of birch limbs, the snap
of candle oil, something was already gone, rushed
past, picked up the heavy bag, I, myself
set down. Should have just
run away, taking all I had
tucked inside the duffel pockets

years ago: Burning places I called home.
Buried names of the dead.
A pointed red calf hide snow hat my sister ties under my chin
in a cold Munich toy shop window, lighting another
small body, shiny porcelain hands, blush
cheeks, glass eyes that open
only if someone holds her.
And my grandmother's Butterick catalog

full of torn pages, the ribbon embroidered
Basque, veil, corset, and lace
tablecloth, sweet warm milk-thistle bread, her favorite
muddy white yard duck, who never did cotton much

to children, those curious black bead
eyes held up like hematite rosary
stones hung on a bureau mirror
above gold encased ointments, charcoal

shadows, lips blotted on a crocheted doily,
my mother's abandoned
costume jewelry box, the secret compartment lost
somewhere in her mind
above all thorns, through all clouds.

Ithaca Commons

Hours begin slowly, unburdening Sola Gallery
ceramic woman, peeling, or is she growing
tenacious clay flesh over street brick; which is it?

If earth recalls nourishment, buried warrior
placenta, Indian paintbrush pollen, the elk
carcass and eventual buzzard, this kiln firewoman

heart, wrist, pulse must be all movement, felspar
road skin breathing in human pain, new river silt
belly, breast, nipple constellation, freed stars

falling from the book where they were called tiny points
on a line, imprisoned too close to speak, unable to feel
anything but the slightest touch, water and breath.

White Cross Doors

Intentional silence. It is time
to recognize the part you play
in your own past.

How old that decision appears, half
discarded, half
preserved, gnawed away
like useless gray rope

hung on a rusted nail peg
hammered into crumbling
stall sills overlooking the broken weave
apple basket, the deliberate lean of broom handle
into a corner inside

this otherwise abandoned barn, where
leather tallow lingers heavy
among the absent
tack, browbands, flank cinches, braided
split reins, that half breed

Elk Mountain breast collar, tapaderos,

black muck, pitched hay dust light falling
through roof breaks.

Who left you behind, who swept away
perfect webs from the trusses and beams
one last time, board-latched
double doors, listened to thunder shake
tin, water running down to the creek
that no longer trickles behind the house.

Who are you? I know someone is here.

THE EXCITEMENT

...All nature, all formations, all creatures exist in and with one another, and they will be resolved again into their own roots...

Mere Bridge

And now the gift returns, liquid silver beads
and links, tiny centers

sinew-threaded, hand-quilled brain-cured hide.
I dare you to stand

on the rock ledge overlooking Susquehanna
valley spirits, crossing

the once green field color that belongs now
to the metal beam bridge

mountain, appearing through fog to hold
the face of this river

edge, listening to the secret of cut glass: perfection
is not for the eye, alone.

At Thirteen

It is evening all afternoon. There is a clock
ticking in the hall, in the doorway, in her room,
and she can't sleep at night anymore. I see
a scratch on her glasses, the wings open and close

but I can't see through them. I don't know
what to do. It is raining and it is going to rain.
There is no river here, no bird or black shadow,
no man or woman of three minds, only this

daughter, sinking into the eye that moves
alone among too many mountains, barbaric
inflections, glass fear to pierce her wrist, mark
the edge of a circle I can't enter, like a tree

apart, whose limbs are torn away to witch water
too far underground to hear magic,
or my heart walking around outside by itself.
I don't care about anything else. I never

wanted to write thirteen ways of staring
outside through long window icicles.

The whistling of a black bird, or just after, mean
nothing at all without her.

Jamie, Rain Season

Let me borrow a spool for your heart
unwind thread white tendons
unravel transcendent lace
coffin veil stitches, row after row
through rosette knots, flesh pigment, greasepaint
museum wax face contusions, hidden river
bruises, broken flash flood sediment
Jack Daniels or Snapple bottle
neck laceration, water mortis
lachrymae mask.

Let me revise your smallness
outside that fitted box world, turn down
the blanket seam your fingers curl gently around,
in a delicate chronicle
of nothing real except chance that was choice.
Colesville Road closed hours, centuries
before they moved the barrier
and drove through flooding rain
while you slept

in the back seat. Washed away

even before that day you stand

in my kitchen and in the corner of my eye

I see you shiver again

so I warm your hands in mine, give you

my son's coat, one more

chocolate chip cookie and a juice box

but still, you look so hungry, so cold, so alone.

Seven Sermons of the Rappahannock

It seems a good day to walk, still cool,
the river current and metal swings, quiet diamonds
soon to be peopled with little league
candy wrappers, last year's
plastic bottles and grocery bags
clinging to chain links
the way particles of self
not everyone can see
die before us, lingering

as we must appear from above, stagnant,
discarded, cave stone implements, flint, mica
water damaged attic oil portraits, cobwebbed
bronze cast hands of an infant
who breathed long enough to cry once,
ears and toes dried by jungle or desert
sun, trophies cut, collected, strung
with fire twine, witnesses Elijah foretold, boy
on the back porch, faceless
kitchen corner girl, ghost chariots
and carved stallions
riding the endless carousel

circle race, metastatic

pavilion windows to that song

coming from somewhere inside the hollow man

sitting alone on a bench, who lifts his eyes to us.

The question there is why

paint fantastic wild-eyed stallions and soldiers,

when so many children

go hungry?

Breast Cancer Pleroma

She collects paper scrap name drawings, fireball cellophane
slips, white lettered spearmint gum stick chains, balsawood
airplanes, many-colored miniature plastic clothes-pinned
in packing-twine flight, tacked
window to window in her bedroom.

He gathers ventriloquist eraser crosses, skin rubbed into scars,
keloidal suicide songs, nirvana pink hair dye, germ spike
ear and brow pierces.

The list grows, writing inside out from its own center.
The choice is between doctor and dinner. It seems
the harder I try the faster I disappear. Still, they preserve
notions of me, anticipate duplicate patterns

and punctures, planes
that never move, hot sweet
arrow scents, torn paperless
letters, indecipherable
lyrics, body trinket
wounds healed open, as if

already they see
how I will look
when I am
gone.

Vigil

Whenever she speaks
I hear her words sound far away
like memory, imprint, fragile stem
leaf veins pressed to a sheet, folded flat on a page
inside a book she carries
to Sterling and Arlington Cemetery plots,
father mother sister caskets aloft

red clay rectangles
sharp spade cut into Virginia summer
brown grass. I just want this to be over, she says,
and I see heat waves above greener clumps
my mother always stops to inspect, bending down
mid-procession, a sudden search I judge to be out of place,
awkward and cold-hearted

or at least inappropriate
like her laughter at her sister's last
Fort Belvoir Hospital bed gasp. But I know now, I was wrong.
Her laughter, even then, flows from the side of suffering.
Wherever she walks, there must be just one
four-leaf clover, somewhere

in the back yard or along the parking lot
edge, twenty years ago now at our Bull Run Park
family reunion; one magic answer folded and hiding, dappled
in patio spearmint, rooted beneath Japanese Quince
outside her laundry room window; one lucky leaf among endless
dandelion globes she digs

with an old steak knife left over
from a set she bought with Green Stamps; one delicate
four leaf clover unlike all others, face down or up. But the leaf
never grows, never shows itself
to her, there is only one triumphant transplant
inside the book she carries now, the bathroom mirror glance
at herself, vodka dripping from the V05 shampoo bottle
where she hides her slow death, her symmetrical lobe
desiccation, her world of words, where

nothing green grows, and
spirit is flesh; flesh, spirit.

Next Door

Ellie appears at the kitchen window
to ask if I will help guide her mother
down the porch stairs.
I didn't know she was home for the day
and I was afraid to ask anyone why
there were so many cars in her driveway.
Helen sits quietly in her lawn chair
with a rainbow colored lifting strap
tied around her chest, surrounded
by backyard perennials, newly planted
every spring since the last world
war.

Lovey, I say, we have missed you so much.
Helen turns to me, and smiles.
I'm going home Friday, she says.
From Ellie's passenger seat
Helen looks out one last time
at the yard angels, potted marigold
seed heads, Madonna's
blue veil peeling as she leans
against the rusted chain link fence

where the gray lamb's ear stalks
begin to fall over along the driveway
Helen must have walked across
unassisted thousands of times.

I put my hand to the car window. Helen
reaches up. We touch
through the watermark that is
my face and the climbing roses
suffering dry heat waves in the glass. I remember
another untouchable rose
my mother kept on the coffee table

suspended inside a water-filled crystal ball
—and those eyes, so distant.

After the train whistle, 2:45 a.m.

I keep the little life
hidden inside a McDonalds happy meal bag
on the top shelf in my closet. The hero
murmurs but makes no cry. I check him
quietly, uncrumpling the paper bag
and carefully loosening his plastic wrap.

When he moans
I hurry back down to the living room
to see if the sound was audible.
To my relief
no one else
heard a thing. After some time, I think

maybe I should slip upstairs to feed him
just a little.
I lock the door behind me,
take down the bag, uncover
the tiny child-man
I hold up to my breast, knowing

he is already dead. How cruel of me

to forget on purpose
the plastic bodied
action figure Jesus or G.I. Joe, whatever
the dream means him to resemble, perhaps

father of all
I hide and starve, who
must never know milk.

SEVEN POWERS

...It flew in the likeness of an eagle, the king of all birds; it flew and alight beside me, and became all speech...

Sacramento

I just sold my mother's diamond ring
to pay for last month's heat.

This is no parable
wrestling angels with golden bows.

The lesson here must be
the terrible hymn of a pearl
become dust, too long bereft

of human touch, disintegrated
into its own dry weight
like the rising number of tent dwellers

sorting through
thin
garments
down
to the bottom
of the last supper city
mission bin: finding nothing to fit, just

one lost pearl, broken loose
from its button place.

We hold only this truth
self-evident, a bauble
crushed in the palm of our hand, stand
together, alone, wonder

who will lift us up?
We are suddenly wise
who find nothing left to pawn.

Return

One last time, every day, go
home again, look
for our lake, black
forest clock, 1848
oak upright piano, my grandmother's cameo
rocker, the marble chessboard with two glass
pawns missing. My daughter and son

wait in the truck. I follow
grass tire tracks, your mud boot
prints into the back
door, garlic sweat
yellow white walls leaning
into their own embrace: window, stairs, window,
I walk, each moment trying not to remember

what happened here, why
we stayed so long, why
we are leaving now. Skeleton light trips

into the attic, tips over the one box
you left behind: baby shoes I collect and carry, room

to room back down to the porch, to rain
on the old slate walkway,
and that black and white photograph
I always stop to pick up.

Reading

After the last time you will ever
touch me again, I run upstairs to the attic
and slash deep lines into drywall, charcoal fingers sift and draw
her hair back into a chignon; the palette knife
loosens untame strands mocking her lace collar: she is
Virginia Woolf and I am afraid I'll never get out
of my own room, so I scratch
pentimento laugh lines and that nose!
Lillian Hellman's: "What was here for me once;
what is here for me now?"

When she is done, I find Emily's madness
divinest sense but prim pose captive, so I lather acrylic
froth at the mouth anger she could not speak,
color the white hands resting in her lap
brown sycamore and burnt umber, and the brush cuts in
secret-sentence dash-laceration, th is - n e w - g a s h - o n-our-lips
floor to ceiling in a portrait charcoal sketched
in microcosmic lipstick embers carried cold
from the bonfire ash circle

I will never forget, this 4ʰ of July Ring of Fire

when each house lights one flare on the lake edge
and each year I wonder, who is looking down
at our signal; who is looking up

through the lake and the eyes of these women
following me across the room, one book at a time
from the pine limb shelf nailed into the northernmost attic wall,
piercing the vault ceiling shadow roof trusses and window bars,
that Victorian birdcage and porcelain dove
I will sell for $50, gas for the truck I will drive across the lawn
two years later, one August morning, when I finally leave?

Time

After he calls and hangs up, I commence to clean, vigorously, without taking a breath: dusting bookshelf, window and sill, TV screen; vacuuming stairs, curtains, plaster walls; tooth brushing toilet crevices, sink overflow drains, grout between every tile, upstairs and down; adjusting chairs to their appropriate table distance and apartness; nudging towels and paper stacks into conformative rectangle edge piles. Once again the bell itself, saliva drips terry cloth and paper, letterhead upon letter, summons and summons, consent to the agreement he writes, interprets, translates into year after year cornerstone justice and justices rising up, block after block until finally something falls from the cabinet shelf: Homer Laughlin platter, teacup, silverware, saucers, yesterday's Virginia Rose pattern.

The walls launch Kindergarten photograph frames and that day, riding away in the car with my mother down Braddock Road, where soldiers in fatigues connect little league baseball field lights, then lightning: electric ladder leap, hash brown grease, the only survivor directs traffic, and I almost fall out of the station wagon passenger door, but he leans into my window, ashen face, eyes bleeding, one red tear falls on my hand: Please keep moving, he says, but China crashes to the floor; my house breaks in two, raising the corner section, triumvirate cement, one arrow vertical, pointed up to the past, that

Livonia Rotary Clam Bake question, may I please have five dollars for a box of tampons? Oh, God. The look on their faces: I am his Smithsonian Medical Museum Elephantiasis Leg, or maybe Little Crow's Head suspended inside a formaldehyde filled jar.

Vertical, without arms to carry dust, a crocheted string for convenient retrieval when skin peels, or when it is time to begin wondering if my dark white headache belongs to those skeletons down where the cement corner was: terrible bones, overrun by carpenter ants, potato bugs, kitchen window wood-boring bees, someone's father burning the moment I wish mine dead for his gin bloodshot eyes, breath, hands on the Indian girl beaten and raped, found naked, knife-splayed under a nameless bridge in a year I can't remember, but here is the other bone woman, huddled against where the hinged door should be that is missing from an old ceramic oven. If you stand very still, sometimes they move. See? That girl and fetus woman, each one, eating her own ghost, bruises and all.

Jesse

Gypsy light, crosswind,
the same question over and over
again, sun burned into skin, pretty
river glass polished in brown sand, then
unearthed among the torn

ghost cups, anonymous styrofoam
litter, moonfish, tiny spider
conch shells, every found and tossed back
pebble sifted from sand
through my hands, collected
in pockets of graphite and ink
uprooted ever since the Potomac
whispered, Run Away, it's a trick

And I let the trick play on my own eyes,
sad fire-keepers, guiding the woman
you could not have known
I would become, strong and winter wild,
but smaller than a star, quiet

and still, right there, waiting for the night
you might look up, just once
remember, wish.

Carrion

The Question Mark lives through winter, feeding
on false nettle, tree sap, pepperbush, dung,
carrion. Green and Gray Commas
sometimes survive bitter cold, too.
But there is just one season of flight
for the Indian Skipper, one spring
for Appalachian Azure to imbibe blackberry, phlox

and viper's bugloss, and only the Common Wood Nymph
understands the shelter and depth of grasses.
These are the wings I followed, eyespots
that rise up to flee and return, thousands
numbering the air when you cross the stream footbridge
from the old field, wading through anonymous weeds
all the way back to the mountain cabin
where the Brown Virgin lies

pinned to a wallboard. I stood in that ragged-winged
light and watched you walk away,
year after year, choosing
not to abide the rule of season, always
searching for the words that would be your last.

When your own mother died, pastor's sermon told the story
of those who wait excitedly for us to arrive
on the other side of wherever it is you were bound to go,
and you marked his sermon well.

But all that time you were trying to die, I waited right here,
already departed from the path you chose. So it is
that I remained, while you flew blind, flung your gift
into the spathe, drawn by the doctrine of signatures
that tendrils and leafs the fragrant lure
of flesh, of the word, your violet eyes
at the moment they begin
rotting: *Home*, you said just before you died,
and I heard our grandmothers sing
through light shaft pierced cloud
Look: Here she comes. Here she comes!

Hierophant

At the end, wave begets wave, ghost foothills
light quiet candles, mist incense

clouds embrace lake child voices, retrace
lonely gray stones amid stones to find one pebble

scuffed into grass, one tongue ablaze overhead
where tempera flames scorch newsprint, finger-paint

bonfire smoke curls above the brand, remembering
the random meaning of signs: coals heaped

and smoldering, twilight welding water and moon
into one horizon smear, palm to heart, iron singed

hands plunged into lake waters again and again
when paper burns inside newly blown glass, waiting

for the promised gathering, but only stillness arrives.

WRATH

...At its voice and the sound of its rustling, I started and arose from my sleep. I took it up and kissed it, and I began to read it according to what was traced on my heart ...

Nymphalis Antiopa

What you call knowledge. Straight-Pinned
to a naming board. Hibernaculum. Aestivate.

Brush-footed. Cryptic brown cloak. How
does it feel to find her missing, then first

to arrive? Black white edge cobalt eye
punctuation you thought forever stilled, alive

in the season beyond survival, where darkness
sent to kill gathers heat, basking in sun on snow,

gnawing through willow, cottonwood, paper
birchbark, Gold Street elm ghost limb leaf

shadows, single-breasted night perforations, wish
bone-pierced lips, the tremolo unsayer who breaks

opacity, perplexes classification, dissects wood-
grain, adhesive labels, the number of pins dancing

on the head of a Monarch who carries milkweed

toxin to Painted Lady and Pearl Crescent. Predator

truth consumes beauty and falls dead. I spin
sterling silk prayer box pendants, dialect, Tunghead

Stonefly lures, Cremaster hooks for hall of justice
mirrors who capture mirrors, and nothing more.

Wet Cement

We used to write
apples, dance core seed circles
around autumn trees
at the edge of Lake Geneva
where minnow fin shadows
stir words into water
spin pebbles into willow sound pools.
parking lot English Daisies
into dry dead stems and seed heads
pressed on blacktop

Now, too many women
are crying on 34th Street
Paper bodies flutter
breathing Fulton name dust
stand in a circle of nothing
underneath Marginal Avenue
where the rats begin to think themselves

poets, spectators
and politicians, build platforms, steal fire
that does not belong to them, forget

the homeless, awaken the idle

bite into disaster

over and over again

until in the place of all language

infinite lies

Ivan's Wake

Walk to the bleachers behind our high school
where Susquehanna storms
Ty Cobb field, spreading brown silt, floating
garbage cans, plastic bags and soda bottles.
Look at that bicycle wheel, that lone
leather sole, the stinking black spot: a dark-furred
god knows what
mingling with toxic chemicals.
This was once a booming factory town.
Some of us stitched those spit-shine boots
the river dredges up and un-seams.
We oiled the fighter planes, riveted
the wings, who now witness this fallen cargo
we became, the almost living snake, beaver, trout
carcass bloating and shredding multi-million dollar
Astroturf. But no one else notices that body

I can see clearly as it arrives curdled up against
one corner of a cement stairwell
at my feet, having traveled and lost, caught
unaware, the corpse appears
fatted from its rich diet, a spoiled town pet,

that river rat I am drawn to

as it seems drawn to me the moment

I lean over the fence, look into his flat open

critter eyes, unable to resist, I touch

the space between the eyes, that glistening

matted scalp of the dead rat, whose frozen pointed

muzzle bare teeth gasp gurgles and sinks, clawed feet

stuck running motionless, still hungry

unaware of his own death.

Crystal Aspersoria

Life in an old house. Sink dishes.
Flooded basement laundry. Two children.
Three Jobs. Exhausted
eleven O'clock death repeats.
And to think, we are all little more than water,
sun and moon tideways,
tinajas, Semiramis's
hanging garden falls.
Marble and sandstone terrace paint, seeping
into ourselves: faience
who flow and evaporate
wood-fired yellow, red, black
glaze, etched scar conquest maps, tattered
sleep, lonely porcelain
rooftop snow, guttural
icicles moaning
tinker's weed bouquet root thirst, ocean
window village light droplets
merging bleak
furnace incense, frozen
steeples, night mountain bishops, empty
white bowls dripping dark

lantern cities, bullets
and arrows, walking

corpses, crackled wet ruins, rain-swollen
rough-hewn arm splinters

fallen but floating, a substance
sprinkled on leftovers, drained.

She Must Have a Name

Story furrowed forehead, black
brow penciled, fable red lip liner, dark
printer's ink—maybe these are things
the woman at Wendy's thinks about, appearing here
as she appears whenever I am in town, waiting
at every deli and fast food counter for an order
mistake, dressed in brown stains, denim,

yellowed Kmart sneakers, the torn blue
cardigan without buttons, wearing her
gray hair, unwashed
but parted and combed, stray
wisps, lost light, lost wisdom.
Mother of God—Maybe
she knows how a single word can thin

and break, dull bone knife split
shoulder to shoulder, leaving one heretic
lock untouched since birth, one last
connection to language
of the first world that was the color
of mother veils, tapestry moth

holes, cashmere larvae
wiggling on mud, one long night
when there is no burger made wrong.

I give her my dinner.
She looks right through me,
and finds an empty table.

Salvaged Limbs, Atlas Skeleton ~ for Ruth Stone

Macular Degeneration. What to do with so much
ardent gray, unaffected sidewalk squares, sandboxes
without perimeter, forlorn
sky paper, one blot spreading blur
into blank. Isn't this a nest upside down?
Print contracture, eye spasms erase appropriate
distance, equate
intricate lace portals
to window glass, one climbing rose
lattice diamond to village block. I know
the mechanism, synaptic lens
openings, poison seeping
into water, fluoride bathing the old
fieldstone foundations, feeding cinderblock
mold roots, ascending
basement stairs, settling into pores, into
marrow. A school playground girl
falls from the monkey bars. Compound fracture.
Metastatic Osteosarcoma, dead calcium
Indian Point Tooth Fairy Studies
call Strontium-90.
And now, over there in the desert

low level radioactive shells
litter the dry air. Even before they are born, children
collect what is left behind. Bellies swell, chemical
teeth cut through
pink gums, lesions, tumors, lymph,
skeleton atlas burqa, soldiers
flown home, who breed
and bear tiny flipper arms and legs, uncounted
fingers and toes never to climb
or fall.   And they say I can't see.

Indelible Guardian

I say please. I say I'm sorry
when it is not my fault. I say God, someday
someone will find me and maybe then you will believe.
But the believing is always after and always too late.
You will never know my name
or the color of my eyes. It is already
too late for me. I am the one standing still
when a rush of crowd side-steps, numb
to such momentary annoyances
as flattened cigarette butts
and gum, bubbled spit, dead women
chalk circles on cement. You just go on
walking down Court Street, more dead than me, past
billboards that flaunt wife-beater
t-shirted men lurking behind
Victoria's Secret. What do you care? After all,
I am the same old story. Why didn't she just leave?
But remember this: I can see you.
Look at the sky beyond those signs
you take into language without question
the way you notice bruises under dark glasses but say
nothing. And every time

you look away, shake the hand
that raises welts on her face, say
what a nice guy he is, order him another martini
and less child support for the road, you set
another empty dinner table, morning hunger
that doesn't dare eat a piece of toast
her daughter might want. You become unfillable space,
page after page
upside down desperate copper dropped into glass,
pennies saved inside the old
peanut butter and jelly jar, mother and children, those few
who survive, the many like me who count
and watch over and tend the untamable, until
it grows strong, and the time comes
for the story
to set out on its own, to find you.

Daughter, Mother, Hospital Woman, Who Wraps Our Bodies?
~ for S.

Finding no news of her murder, no story
to explain what happened, I decide
I am weary of the handprint
scar around my throat, damn tired
like everyone else
of strangulation, of flowers, of sending
checks to a women's shelter, in lieu.

Dear friend, no one wants to hear
any more. And so, the silence grows
until there are no words
left, where you sit alone tonight
in that corner chair, awaiting your own
daughter's funeral, no difference
between survivor and dead, wrapped
in a dark room blanket, perhaps
not yet knowing who

could take a daughter's life, and why
if there is such a thing
as why. Or maybe

you know exactly who he was, knew
all along it would come to this
long blank hallway leading
to a heavy door, a clipboard
list, the mark beside her name, the proper
drawer slid open, or the border
of yellow tape, lifted for you

to walk underneath, the echo
that will always follow to her body,
recall the first bruise, the first
stitches, the shy new shoes for her
first day of school, the clatter
of utensils, the search for a wooden
spoon to stir cookie batter, scissors
to cut seedbed twine, her first recipe, first
marigold, first place blue ribbon, mama

look, she cries, no hands, mama
watch me dive, count how long
I can hold my breath.

Near Munich, I was born

Only one witness lived, just long enough
to smuggle this four and a half minute PBS film
out of Afghanistan. There is a convoy of trucks,
commandeered, packed with men
sealed into steel shipping containers that look like
freight train cars. The prisoners cry out for air. The soldiers
shoot holes through the metal, quieting some. Others
survive by licking sweat from the sick, bite and drink
the blood of the wounded who must stand
pressed against sun heated container walls.

The distance is 120 kilometers
to Sheberghan Prison, where American soldiers
open the convoy containers, cover their own faces
with medical masks, try
not to breathe feces, urine, vomit,
rotting flesh, as they search and seize
identification papers from 3000 they accompany
back to the desert near Dascht-I-Lelie, that is now

a place of bones, shreds of clothing
with Pakastani labels, bullet shells, sand,

and while I watch that film, snow settles
on a mountain, a fence, cement buildings
with ovens open and black inside
at eye-level, so I can't be more than four
or five years old and still I look up
to ask my father

Why did you bring me here? How can anyone say
we did not know what happened to those people?

Shariah Court, Honor Killing

Those condemned
to stoning, who escape and run away
are allowed to go free, according to law.
The man must be
buried up to his waist. The woman
to her neck.

A stone is defined thus:
nothing so large as to cause death
upon only two or three blows; nothing
so small
as to be no longer considered a stone.

The people shout
God is Great. Adulteress, even if
you manage to dig your way out
women are always caught again.
Hundreds are reburied.

Better to kiss the boy
weaned early for your execution; step
down quietly into the ditch; arrange

your linen garment, silk veil, arms
folded, one hand
upon each breast, until

bystanders fill the pit
and dust settles; the boy's cry
lets down your milk, your blood
into the earth that used to be our mother.
It is his right after all,
to bear witness.

Dark Energy, Dark Matter

Stars are no longer thought
to be tiny. Something permeates
imaginary barriers, crushes
from within carbon, the basis and building block
of life, Particulate Energy
Einstein called the Dark Constant, a quintessence
forcing galaxies apart, accelerating bodies forever
toward the big rip, bound

to tear through planet, galaxy, Bethlehem
star stuff, crowded
cafés, library doors, the back
of a green bus, exploding
cosmological content, dark matter
that dwells in the emptiest space between
pieces of iron, glass, heart. In grief
the bystander says

I felt blood on my head.
I saw terrible things.
I tried not to look.
And so—we, who misunderstand

gravity, rebuild razor wire fences

no one dare say, recall

snow in summer, hollow

eyes, incalculable

ash, lice, typhus, trenches

around an approach

that never arrives, the severed arm

tattoo, intricate lampshade number sequences

naming hourglass nebulae, coiling a collapse

even light cannot escape.

Six Finger Lakes

It will rain today. Again.
Lakebeds, the great mystery
handprint, fills
terrible new drop offs. No sign

appears to warn or calm.
Thunder persists without lightning.
Storms of late summer
abandon covenant, arise mid-sun,

flaunt reckless heat scrabble
word waves on air, cast
letterless bone
pellets to asphalt: a forest become

weed creviced black desert,
prayer flags revised into veiled rock
women ordered to lie
face down before soldiers, who
cradle machine guns.

How primitive they are, one says.

Some of them don't even have shoes.

What have we done
with the arc of promise,
the quiet olive twig, the remembering
to look up?

V. Priceana, The Violet Age

Bodies I step over
number more than I can count.
They are all the same life color, leaping up
and dying again. All, except one. God,
she is beautiful, the little girl
I find in the midst

of death, unable to speak
the name of her mother.
She wears a torn wildflower
print dress, no shoes
on the tiny feet dangling from my hip
somewhere in the past
when I carry her to someone
I hope has a better chance of escape.
I think of her every day,
keep the watercolor tree she painted
folded up, pressed in my book, wonder if
she ever made it out alive.

Last night I dreamed
I am both

waiting and arrived, two women
and one child,
I, myself, bring back and hold
between us, soft violet hair
the same laugh, black dove
eyes, crescent light centered.

Unpacking the Bread Knife

The always careful miracle, this time
cut just a little too deep, a message in hand
that can never be
sent back. Here lies the final lesson,
the first law of fire, someone
you love, whose name disappears inside
a tall boy chest, one last morning
collection of rings, fat brown whiskey
glasses, the leather wallet and cross
pen, crumpled dollars, fuzzy lint, coins
clumped on a Days Inn
Front Street, Binghamton
note pad, that black puzzle

of pocket things, looking out
through bedroom window blinds,
blade and light alternating
for three years now, carving a face

destined to become
the negative relief
palm-grip linoleum block

never blue India ink dipped, never

blotted and pressed to cotton paper,

a serrated absence you, too, hold

by the neck, shove against a wall, slap

backhanded until the lips crack, bleed

into a cardboard box

dropped among other kitchen things

that scrape, stir, scar,

take up too much space, make

too much noise.

Creator Hourglass

When I am old I might
fall down between perennial garden border
train ties, scrape skin from my ankle and knee, rest
my wrinkled cheek on uprooted cosmos crushed into
morning damp earth, dozing while I wait.
And if no one happens by, I suppose
I'll just laugh at that dirt clod stuck between my toes,
close my eyes and rest
until I can stand again, lighted on that highest dune
I am afraid to climb when I am seven,
find one half oyster

shell, there in the heart pocket
of my favorite cut-off overalls, where I tuck the shell
all those years ago as a child
sifting through sea oats below Kill Devil Hills, wide-eyed
at the sight of shipwreck horses swimming abreast
storm surf, black wildflower manes
rising out of breakers, where the last red woman
takes my hand before walking away
down that timeline trail I retrace
now: rawhide strung coral

dancing memory into survival, blood
divided into a fraction
equal to the number who died, running here
and there, tower to tower, wave after wave
of sand over castles
built and swallowed, sorrow
cut from the skin of hope, discovery
learning from its past
how not to destroy
windflowers and barefooted feathers.

On a rain drop, Morning

Bulbs and switches spark
one by one, to black. We have
no working ceiling light. Our house
falls down-nail by nail around us; rotted
floorboards creak to each footstep.
The furnace flinches on and off.
I don't know

how to fix broken things, find
enough money to pay the high cost
of living in America. Night sweat
lies awake, renewing the age
of child factories, Indian boarding
schools, dust bowl grapes, kitchen table
abortions, Baptist Church

bombs, Pacification Teams, the girl child
Life Magazine naked scream
black and white dirt street rice paddy
that is now mud brick someone calls home.
But I have a dream
that still terrifies dress blue

doorbell messengers, dark suit café
meetings after work, belly-wound-blood
desert cocktails, lip corners dripping
chemical content. I think they test
for water made into stone, travertine
terraces, a woman writing alone
who will soon bake enough bread

to feed the hungry. Already
the rising begins.

Blood Mountain

Everyone is gone now. It is getting cold.
The gray haired man dresses neatly in jeans
and a black shirt, packs a small bag and tucks it
behind the driver's seat. Somewhere, he pulls off
the road at a diner, orders meatloaf
and mashed potatoes.

Written in blue pen on his right hand, an old poem
smudges where knuckles bend the poem's line
breaks. His hand shakes. The fork drips
wrought iron pan gravy
liverspots on gaudy red formica.
She never painted her fingernails.

On the counter, an unfolded map
fades, fluorescented blue rapids follow a dotted trail
all the way to a pencil circle drawn around that peak.
His fingertip shadow recalls the cleft
in the small of her back. Beautiful man, she said
when he touched her there.

At the summit, Blood Mountain
Yunwee-chuns-dee sing magic songs
echoing from their tiny caves. Red lichen bless
the old battleway. Nunnehee stitch clouds together
into a warm quilt. They fit together precisely
as they were made to do.

I was wrong. It was perfect, his Chahta eyes
decide, settled far below on a single pebble
turned on its back, a low belly moan washed clean,
revealing the polished skin of a name
slipping along clay sediment, clawing up
riverbank to treeline arms to sky to that ledge
face of the great rock, wailing.

fin

About The Author

Elizabethe Kelley is an Associate Professor at The Sage Colleges in Troy, New York. A writer, storyteller and educator, Elizabethe's research, writing and artwork appears in cutting-edge creative and critical regional, national and international publications in print and online. She teaches social and environmental justice discourse, storytelling, writing and multi-ethnic rhetorical approaches, including traditional, indigenous modes of communication, teaching and learning.

In both fiction and poetry, her writing inhabits permeable worlds through narrative voices that walk through an Appalachian and Native heritage that is indelible among stories so often excluded from the history of American culture. This collection of poems calls together another journey familiar to writers, traversing ancient through contemporary texts, so that writing, itself joins into a conversation with the past that is always before us, awaiting a future we cannot see from within our own cocooned human experience.

Acknowledgments

"Sacramento." <u>Lady Jane's Miscellany</u>. Anthology. Mac McKinney, Ed., San Francisco, CA & Norfolk, VA: San Francisco Bay Press, Summer 2010.

"We Live Here." <u>Red Line Blues: Lean Times</u>. Anthology. Erich Nagler, Moriah Norris-Hale & Benjamin Yanes, Eds., Brooklyn, NY & Asheville, NC, February 2010.

"Crystal Aspersoria." <u>Red Line Blues: Lean Times</u>. Anthology. Erich Nagler, Moriah Norris Hale & Benjamin Yanes, Eds., Brooklyn, NY & Asheville, NC, February 2010.

"Jesse." <u>(Dis)Comfort Zones</u>. Issue 23. Blue Print Review. Independent Press Online. Dorothee Lang, Ed., Berlin, Germany, January 2010.

"Variola Fever." <u>Triggerfish Critical Review</u>. Independent Press Online. Brendan McEntee, Ed., December 2009.

"Blood Mountain." <u>Writer's Block</u>. WebZine. Teilo Moore and Ben Gehrels, Eds., Canada, December 2009.

"What Silence Means." <u>SUSS Literary Journal</u>. Dan Manchester, Ed., New York: Black Lawrence Press, Winter 2009.

"Sacramento." <u>New Verse News</u>. James Penha, Ed., March 2009. Pushcart Prize Nomination, November 2009.

"Vigil." <u>Trillium Literary Journal</u>. Online, Coleman Myron, Ph.D., Ed., Alexandria, VA: Alexandria Press, February 2009.

"Shariah Court Honor Killing." <u>CONTE: Journal of Narrative Writing</u>. June 2008.

"Carrion Vine Butterfly." Tonopah Review: A Quarterly Journal of Prose & Poetry. July 2008.

"Aces, Eights & Hearts." Origami Condom Literary Magazine. Issue #8. Kenneth P. Gurney, Ed., June 2008.

"Anna, Did You Write?" Origami Condom Literary Magazine. Issue #8. Kenneth P. Gurney, Ed., June 2008.

"Broome County Courthouse, Irelu's Song for Ilargia." Earth's Daughters. Kastle Brill, Ed., Buffalo, NY, Spring 2007.

"On a rain drop, Morning." HazMat Review. Norm Davis, Ed., Rochester, NY: Clevis Hook Press, Spring 2007.

"Grandmother's Road." Poems for the Mountains. Wizansky, Margot, Ed., Boston: Salt Marsh Pottery Press, Spring 2006.

"What Lies Here After Fourteen Years." For Better or Worse. Anthology. Bonita Sutterby, Ed. New Smyrna: PoetWorks Press. ISBN 1-930293-47-X, Fall 2005.

"Lilly Lake." For Better or Worse. Anthology. Bonita Sutterby, Ed., New Smyrna: PoetWorks Press. ISBN 1-930293-47-X, Fall 2005.

"Thimbleweed Aphasia." For Better or Worse. Anthology. Bonita Sutterby, Ed. New Smyrna: PoetWorks Press. ISBN 1-930293-47-X, Fall 2005.

"Unpacking the Bread Knife." For Better or Worse. Anthology. Bonita Sutterby, Ed. New Smyrna: PoetWorks Press. ISBN 1-930293-47-X, Fall 2005.

"Shariah Court, Honor Killing." For Better or Worse. Anthology. Bonita Sutterby, Ed. New Smyrna: PoetWorks Press. ISBN 1-930293-47-X, Fall 2005.

"Our Mother's Cookbook." For Better or Worse. Anthology. Bonita Sutterby, Ed. New Smyrna: PoetWorks Press. ISBN 1-930293-47-X, Fall 2005.

"At Thirteen." The Motherhood Anthology. Berkeley, CA: Purple Canary Press. Spring 2005.

"Daughter, Mother, Hospital Woman Who Wraps Our Bodies." Clackamas Review. Spring 2005.

"Letter." FEMSPEC Review. Batya Wienbaum, Ed., Cleveland: FemSpec Press. Spring 2005.

"She Must Have A Name." Ascent Literary Magazine. May 2004.

"Dark Energy, Dark Matter." Red Booth Review. Anthology. W.T. Pfefferle, Ed., Fall 2004.

"Nymphalis Antiopa;" The Antietam Review. Philip Bufithis, Ed., Fall 2004.

"V. Priceana, the Violet Age." Anthology of New England Writers. Frank Anthony, Ed., Fall 2004.

"Near Munich, where I was born." Pedestal Magazine. John Amen, Ed., October 2004.

"Salvaged Limbs, Atlas Skeleton ~for Ruth Stone." Poem. Pedestal Magazine. John Amen, Ed., October 2004.

"The Six Finger Lakes." Pedestal Magazine. John Amen, Ed., October 2004.

"Grandmother's Road." A Nickel's Worth of Dreams. Anthology. Bonita Sutterby, Ed. New Smyrna: PoetWorks Press. ISBN 1-930293-41-0, Fall 2004.

"At the Center, Creator Hourglass." Red, White and Blues, Poetic Vistas on the Promise of America. Ryan G. Van Cleave and Virgil Suarez, Eds., University of Iowa Press, Fall 2004.

"Dark Energy, Dark Matter." Red Booth Review. W.T. Pfefferle, Ed., Online Issue #13, Summer 2004.

"Nymphalis Antiopa." Ellipsis. Westminster College Press, Spring 2004.

"Cure ~ for Adrienne Rich." Icarus International Review. North Carolina State Council on the Arts, Fall 2003.

"Forbidden." The Antietam Review. Philip Bufithis, Ed., Washington County Maryland Council on the Arts, Fall 2003.

"At Thirteen." Anthology of New England Writers. Frank Anthony, Ed., 2003.

"Last of the Lake Pearls." Icarus International Review. North Carolina State Council on the Arts, Fall 2002.

"Mother Poem." The Kali Guide: A Directory of Resources for Women. Stelli Munnis, Ed., Zenprint, August 2002.

"She is Asking." The Kali Guide: A Directory of Resources for Women. Stelli Munnis, Ed., Zenprint, August 2002.

Note on Chapter Heading Quotes:

The italicized excerpts appearing with chapter headings are excerpts of "The Gospel of Mary Magdalene" from the Nag Hammadi codices discovered in Egypt in 1945, which are transcribed and available online through The Gnostic Society Library.

www.ingramcontent.com/pod-product-compliance
Lightning Source LLC
LaVergne TN
LVHW051125080426
835510LV00018B/2238